Blue & White
Pottery

A Collector's Guide

Blue & White
Pottery

A Collector's Guide

Gillian Neale

MILLER'S BLUE & WHITE POTTERY: A COLLECTOR'S GUIDE
by Gillian Neale

First published in Great Britain in 2000 by Miller's, a division
of Mitchell Beazley, imprints of Octopus Publishing Group Ltd,
2–4 Heron Quays, Docklands, London E14 4JP

First published in the U.S.A. in 2000

Miller's is a registered trademark of Octopus Publishing Group Ltd
This edition distributed in the U.S.A. by Antique Collectors' Club Ltd.,
Market Street Industrial Park, Wappingers' Falls, New York, NY 12590, U.S.A.

Commissioning Editor **Liz Stubbs**
Executive Art Editor **Vivienne Brar**
Project editor **Clare Peel**
Production **Nancy Roberts**
Designer **Louise Griffiths**
Indexer **Sue Farr**
Jacket photography by **Steve Tanner**

ISBN 1 84000 287 5

A CIP catalogue record for this book is available from the British Library

Set in Bembo, Frutiger and Shannon
Produced by Toppan Printing Co., (HK) Ltd.
Printed and bound in China

Jacket illustrations, left to right: pair of "Chinese Temples" pattern
knife-rests, 1830; "Bride of Lammermoor" pattern 15cm/6in plate,
1840; jug showing Crystal Palace, 1860; "Blind Boy" pattern
dessert-dish, 1820; restored "Italian" pattern Goose eggcup, 1900

contents

Where to start

Forming a collection, including one of blue-and-white pottery, is a very personal affair. You have to live with and be happy with the collection and its contents. The aim of this book is to guide the new collector through some of the minefield of items available, and to point out possible pitfalls to be encountered along the way.

It may help to start by asking a few basic questions. Where is the collection going to be displayed? Do you have an idea of the design, or type of pattern, you like best? Perhaps you have inherited items of blue-and-white pottery that you wish to add to or match? Or perhaps you simply wish to start from scratch? Cost is usually also an important factor: how much do you want to spend, and how much can you afford?

Having a hands-on approach is probably the best way to learn about antiques, so visit antiques fairs and shops to look at and (carefully) handle items of blue and white. This should help you to establish a good idea of what is on the market, before buying. Find a dealer with whom you feel comfortable, and whom you can trust. Invest time in talking to

dealers – many dealers are also avid collectors, and are only too happy to talk you through their wares. They also have reputations to maintain, and should be willing to help you; if you have to pay a little more than you would at a garage sale, do not begrudge the extra cost, as you are benefiting from the dealer's expertise. If you become a regular customer, this may well work in your favour. You may instantly know what appeals, but do not be deterred if this is not the case – take your time, and do not be rushed into making a purchase that you may regret later. Always buy the best that you can afford, and, importantly, items that you like. Always ask for a descriptive receipt, giving details about the item, and noting any repairs or damage. This is important for both your own protection, and insurance purposes. Collections can grow, and become very valuable, so be sure to include them on your household contents policy.

The examples featured on these pages illustrate several points that can help with what to look out for when starting a collection. The piece shown left is a large platter – sometimes known as a charger, or, in Scotland, as an ashet – produced by Turner at the Lane End pottery between 1800 and 1810; it is decorated with the "Stag" pattern, which shows a stag within a "chinoiserie", or Chinese-style, pattern of willow trees, plants and pagodas – a recurrent theme in blue-and-white pottery. The type of pattern shown is often one of the most important factors with regard to value, so it is a good idea to find out as much as possible about which patterns are most collectible, which are most frequently found, and which are most unusual. The color of the pattern can

also help determine when a piece was made, and, perhaps, by whom. On this platter the blue is very dark, with an almost inky appearance, and this is typical of early 19thC blue-and-white wares. Size is another important factor for value, and this platter is one of the largest available, measuring a total of 52.5cm/21in wide, which increases its value. However, with such large items as this, make sure that you will be able to house them.

If a piece has been restored, this will affect the value, although, on some very rare items restoration may be less detrimental to the value (see pp.58–9). The outer rim of this platter had two small chips, which have been restored

professionally; however, because of the restoration, the platter can only be used for decoration. If it were in perfect condition, this piece would be worth between $640 and $720, but the value is decreased to between $480 and $560 because of the repair.

It is also possible to build up sets over time, as illustrated by the composite toilet-set, in the very popular "Italian" pattern, shown above. Produced by the Stoke-on-Trent-based Copeland factory, between 1890 and 1920, all the items in this set were collected and matched over a number of years – one of the real joys of collecting. So be patient, and enjoy the thrill of looking for that elusive blue-and-white treasure.

Prices & dimensions
The price ranges given in this book should be taken as guides to value only, as value depends greatly on trends in the market place, geographical location, and condition.

Dimensions are given in centimetres and inches, with abbreviations as follows: **diam.** diameter; **ht** height; **l.** length; and **w.** width.

What is blue-and-white pottery?

Patterns in blue and white were first used to decorate ceramics in the 17thC by the Chinese, when they were hand-painted (an expensive process) on to porcelain. Wares decorated in this way became more affordable in the late 18thC, when the more cost-effective process of transfer-printing patterns on to ceramics was introduced.

Transfer-printing

In transfer-printing, an engraver draws a design on paper, which is then traced, and engraved in dots, on to a copper plate. Detail and shading are achieved by varying the depth of the dots – the deeper the dots, the deeper the color. A mixture of ink and oils is applied to the copper plate, which is kept warm to prevent the ink from drying.

The ink-and-oil mixture is forced into the dots, and any excess is scraped off with a palette knife. A strong tissue paper, coated in a mixture of soap and water to allow for easy movement, is then laid on the copper plate, and both are then passed through heavy steel rollers to force every detail of the pattern on to the tissue paper. The paper is then carefully removed from the plate, and passed to the cutters, who trim away any excess. The

◀▲ Platter and original print
This mint-condition platter, which shows the cathedral church, Glasgow, and is from the "Antique Scenery" series, was produced c.1823–30 by an unknown maker, possibly in Staffordshire. It is available in one size only (w. 48cm/19in). A combed back stops it from slipping on a flat surface. Also shown is the original source print, from which the engraving was taken. Prints such as this add to the interest of any collection; however, they are generally more difficult to find than items of pottery.
Platter: **$640–960**; print: **$160–400**

pattern (now in reverse) is placed on the object to be decorated, and rubbed all over with a stiff brush to transfer the pattern. Borders are applied separately.

The decorated article is then soaked in a tub of water, to soften the tissue, and aid its removal. The oil-based color remains unaffected by the water. After drying, the article is biscuit-fired in a kiln, at approximately 1,450 to 1,485 degrees to evaporate the oils, and set the color. The object is dipped into a glaze, and any excess glaze is shaken off, to leave a fine coating over the transfer – hence the process is often referred to as "underglaze transfer-printing."

Sometimes, due to a fault in the glazing process, the blue color flows over the edges of the pattern, giving what is commonly known as a "flow blue" design. Owing to the popularity of flow blue in the last part of the 19thC, this effect was produced artificially, by adding a flow powder to the glaze at the time of firing.

◄▲ "Gem" pattern copper plate

This copper plate, showing the "Gem" pattern, was engraved by the Jamieson factory, in Scotland, between 1836 and 1854. Unusually, both center and border patterns are featured together – borders were usually printed separately. The engraving is well worn, which would mean the pattern would not reproduce successfully. To prolong the life of a copper plate, the pattern was often re-engraved to make it sharper. Copper plates, especially one such as this, with the name of the pattern printed on it as a backstamp, are hard to find. The plate is from the same series, although it is a different size and has a different middle.

Copper plate: **$128–192**; plate **$48–64**

After drying, the transfer-printed items are stacked in "Glost" ovens (see glossary), for refiring at very high temperatures – between 2,260 and 2,330 degrees – to melt the glaze and form a tough, even, transparent coating. All items set in Glost ovens are separated by small pyramids of clay, to prevent them from sticking together, and the small marks left by these pyramids are commonly known as "stilt" marks. The shape of the stilt mark varies from factory to factory, and this can be a great help with regard to identification and dating.

▲ ▼ The wash-bowl, below left, which is part of a toilet set, features the "white-on-blue", all-over "Moss Rose" pattern, and was produced by Minton c.1830. The detail below shows how the transfer is cut and joined, to fit the shape of the object.

Washbowl: **$320–400** (in good condition)

"Broseley" & "Willow" patterns

The "Willow" pattern is the most common blue-and-white design, and many people mistakenly think that all blue and white is "Willow." Introduced in 1780 by Spode, the pattern depicts a love story, of Chinese origin, in which the daughter of a rich man falls in love with her father's secretary, much to her father's horror. The young man is banned from the house, and the father arranges a marriage for his daughter. The lovers elope, and the father decrees that they are to be caught, and put to death. When they are discovered, several years later, the young man is killed, and the young woman sets fire to their house, and dies in the flames. The lovers are reunited in death as two lovebirds. The "Broseley" pattern shows the same story but in a paler blue.

▼ **"Broseley" pattern mustard-pot**

This mustard-pot is printed in the "Broseley" pattern, which is a paler blue than the traditional "Willow" pattern. "Broseley" is also unusual in showing two ornate temples rather than one, and in having the bridge on the right-hand side of the pattern, not the left. Also, there are only two figures on the bridge, not the usual three. This piece is of a lesser quality than the toast rack (above right), and was possibly intended for use by the servants, "below stairs," or for breakfast. The pottery is heavy, and the transfer-printing indistinct. The value reflects the fact that the piece still has its lid.

"Broseley" pattern mustard-pot, 1830, ht 7.5cm/3in, **$96–128**

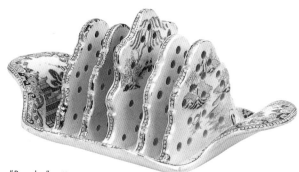

"Broseley" pattern toast rack, c.1830, l. 15cm/6in, **$272–320**

▲ **"Broseley" pattern toast rack**

This fine piece, showing the "Broseley" pattern, was produced c.1830 in Staffordshire, but is not attributable to a particular potter. Toast racks are sought after by collectors, but they should be checked carefully for signs of repair, especially on the uprights and the undersides of the handles. Some toast racks are more oblong than this example; Spode produced one in a boat shape.

Spoon rest, c.1830,
l. 10cm/4in, **$80–160**

▲ Spoon rest

This piece is decorated in the traditional, three-figure "Willow" pattern. Note, however, that only the father's house, and the bridge, are shown, due to the fact that copper plates were not engraved for individual items. Instead, a large transfer was cut to fit a number of objects. The next spoon rest produced may, therefore, have shown only the tree and the fence, or even just the border. Spoon rests are often called pickle dishes, but in fact they were used to rest the serving spoon during a meal. This one was made c.1830 in Staffordshire, by an unknown potter. The thick pottery suggests that the piece was used "below stairs".

▼ Salt-cellar and pepper-pot

This is a "matched" pair (i.e. one that has been put together by a collector), which will affect the value, even though the match is a good one. Unusually, the salt-cellar is decorated with the full "Willow" pattern, not just the border. The pepper-pot has holes around the side, as well as on top. Both pieces were produced c.1830–35, possibly by a Staffordshire pottery.

Salt-cellar and pepper-pot, both c.1830–5; salt ht 5cm/2in, **$64–96**; pepper ht 10cm/4in, **$80–144**

FACT FILE

The "Willow" Pattern

The following elements make up the "Willow" pattern: a willow tree (signifying sadness); a pagoda (the father's house); a small building, to the left of the house (his daughter's prison); a bridge, on which are seen the daughter, her lover, and her father; a boat, with the lovers escaping; the island where they live together; a burning house; the two lovebirds.

"Yorkshire Relish" plate, c.1860, diam. 7.5cm/3in, **$19–32**

▲ "Yorkshire Relish" plate

This rather fun item had a dual function, being made both to advertise "Yorkshire Relish", and to provide a stand for the relish bottle to rest on during the meal. "Yorkshire Relish" was made in Leeds by the firm of Goodalls. The plates first appeared c.1860, and were produced with slight variations in the inscription around the rim.

"Italian" pattern

The ever-popular, "Italian" pattern was introduced by the Spode factory, in Stoke-on-Trent, in 1816. It continued in production after 1833, when the pottery was bought by the firm of Copeland & Garrett, and from 1847 to 1970, under the name of Copeland. The Spode name was reintroduced in 1970, and today "Italian" pattern Spode pottery is still produced in large quantities. The pattern itself was taken from a pen-and-wash drawing of the ruins of the Coliseum in Rome, which can be seen on display at the Spode Museum. The border is a copy of a Chinese Imari-type design. Every conceivable item of pottery has been produced in this pattern, which was also copied by other manufacturers, including Stubbs.

▼ **Chestnut or fruit basket by Copeland**
This piece, with its intricate basketweave design, was originally part of a dessert service, used to serve roasted chestnuts or crystallized fruits. Produced c.1880 by the Copeland factory, in Stoke-on-Trent, it follows the original Spode pattern and shape. At least two baskets were made for each dessert service. Some also have small feet. This type of piece is very vulnerable to damage.

"Italian" pattern chestnut or fruit basket, c.1880, l. 5cm/2in, **$400–480**

▲ **Tea-caddy, and "Crichton" teapot, by Copeland**
The "Crichton" shape was introduced by the Copeland factory in 1879, and was a copy of a red, stoneware Chinese teapot. It was usually inscribed with a quotation based on Burns' *Auld Lang Syne*. On this piece the spout tip (vulnerable) has a restored chip. The tea-caddy has an unusual shape, and is also rare in having its original lid. It carries the same inscription as the teapot. The pieces were made around the same time.

Tea-caddy, and "Crichton" teapot, both 1900–1920; teapot: ht 15cm/6in, **$160–240**; tea-caddy: ht 17.5cm/7in **$480–560**

Container set, 1900–1930,
ht 10cm/4in,
$128–224

▲ Container set

This is a matched
set, the mustard-pot lid
and the spoon being very
rare finds. It is one of several
shapes produced early in the
20thC by Copeland. The stand
has a central looped handle,
rising above the condiments,
and is decorated with the
"Italian" border pattern, as
are the lid of the mustard-pot,
and the mustard spoon. The
mustard-pot, pepper-pot, and
salt-cellar all feature the
full pattern.

MARKS
The oval, underglaze,
printed mark (top) was
used on "Italian" pattern
Copeland ware from 1894
to 1970. The lower mark
was introduced in 1890.

Loving-cup, c.1920,
ht 10cm/4in, **$96–144**

▲ Loving-cup

Loving-cups (two-handled cups
or mugs) were originally given
as engagement or betrothal
presents. Each partner had his
or her own handle, and side
of the cup, to drink from.
Loving-cups come in several
sizes, this being one of the
smallest. Rare examples,
known as "tygs," have three
handles. This cup, which is in
perfect condition, is decorated
on the outside with the full
"Italian" pattern, and at the
top and on the inner rim with
the border pattern. The "Auld
Lang Syne" inscription (see far
left) sometimes appears on
the inner or outer rim.

FACT FILE

Sandwich plate, 1935,
diam. 25cm/10in, **$32–48**

▲ Sandwich plate
by Copeland

Octagonal-shaped plates,
such as this, were produced
in large quantities, for two
to three years from 1934,
by Copeland. They could be
obtained, free of charge, by
collecting ten labels from tins
of "Skippers" sardines. The
plates feature a raised cross in
the center, and a raised rose
decoration around the edge.

"Wild Rose" pattern

This pattern gets its name from its border of dog roses. The central motif shows a river scene, with two punts (possibly a ferry) carrying passengers across a river. A rustic bridge crosses the river, and nearby is a thatched cottage; in the background is a large house. The river is the River Thames, and the house is Nuneham House, near Oxford, the seat of the Earl of Harcourt. The pattern was introduced in 1830 by a large number of factories. The quality of both the pottery and the print can vary greatly, and very few examples are marked with the potter's name. Items for the table are most common, but toilet items are also available. The "Wild Rose" pattern has become increasingly sought after by collectors in recent years.

Shell-shaped dish, c.1830, ht 10cm/4in, **$160–240**

▶ Shell-shaped dish

This shell-shaped dish was made in the 1830s. It is unmarked, and the maker is unknown. Nevertheless, the piece is finely potted, and the transfer is very crisp. The dish was used to serve small pieces of raw fish, such as lumpfish or roe. It may also have been used for cockles, and other shellfish. It is ridged on both inner and outer sides, to resemble a shell, and has three small feet molded in the shape of shells. This shape is not common, which increases the value of the piece. When buying an item such as this, watch for rim chips and cracks along the ridges.

▼ Arcaded plate

This unmarked plate is part of a dessert service; the name comes from the pierced rim added to the basketweave border, which replaces the traditional "Wild Rose" border. Arcaded plates (see p.27) were made to complement dessert baskets and comports, and were used with spoons, rather than knives and forks, so their surfaces are not usually as scratched as those of dinner plates. The molded edges are fragile, and chip easily, but the rims restore well, and often invisibly. To check for repairs, run a finger along the edge. These plates may also be described as "reticulated".

Arcaded plate, c.1830, ht 20cm/8in, **$160–240**

▼ Basket stand

This fine-quality, oval stand was made as the undertray for a chestnut or fruit basket (see p.12), and the edges are formed from large, woven loops. The "Wild Rose" border is visible on the inside of the stand. The transfer used to decorate this piece was originally for a small tureen-base or platter, the border being trimmed to fit the oval shape. As with the arcaded plate shown left, the edge of this piece is very fragile, but in this case the loops are white, and restorations are therefore much easier to spot. This particular stand is in good condition, and its value reflects this. It is unmarked, and the maker is unknown.

Basket stand,1825–35, l. 25cm/10in, **$240–320**

▼ Wash-stand jug

This jug was part of a toilet set; the wash-bowl is now lost. It is not of fine quality, and so is unlikely to have had a copper plate engraved especially for it. The pattern was formed using two transfers, possibly taken from plates, which were wrapped around the jug, joined at the handle, under the spout, and then trimmed to fit. The joins are still visible. These jugs make attractive vases, and are popular with collectors. The potter is unknown.

Wash-stand jug, 1830–40, ht 25cm/10in, **$240–400**

Major manufacturers of "Wild Rose" pottery

- Bell (Glasgow)
- Bovey Tracey (Devon)
- Clementson (Staffordshire)
- Fell (Tyneside)
- Meir (Staffordshire)
- Moore (Sunderland)
- Podmore Walker (Staffordshire)
- Twigg (Yorkshire)
- Wood (Yorkshire)

▼ Cheese or breakfast plate

Originally part of a large dinner-service, this plate has had a very hard life; the edges are stained black, probably the result of its having been left too long in the oven, but there is no other damage. The potting is thick and heavy, although the transfer is very clear. Since it was produced as a "below-stairs" piece, this plate could be displayed on a plate wire without fear of damage to the edges, and, if it were displayed high up, the poor quality would go unnoticed.

Cheese or breakfast plate, 1830–40, diam. 20cm/8in, **$48–64**

"Asiatic Pheasants" pattern

Introduced in the second half of the 19thC by many factories, including Wedgwood, this pattern is second in popularity only to the "Willow" pattern (*see* pp.10–11). It was traditionally printed in a pale blue, and some pieces are much paler than others, causing them to appear faded. However, note that the pattern is overglazed, and cannot fade. The central motif, which does not fill the whole plate, shows a large pheasant, and smaller birds and flowers. The border is composed of flowers. Demand for this pattern, which was once eschewed by collectors, increased in the 1980s, when it was used for a popular range of tableware, also produced in green, pink, and brown.

▼ Round vegetable tureen by Thomas Dimmock & Co.

Round vegetable tureens were produced by Dimmock between 1828 and 1859, and can be identified by their domed lids, and pedestal bases. Many examples have lost their lids, but a small indentation on the rim of the bowl will show where the lid once fitted. The Dimmock mark is seen on the base as an impressed "D," with a "T" on top. The lid is decorated with the "Asiatic Pheasants" border pattern; the full design is seen on the inside of the base.

Round vegetable tureen by Thomas Dimmock & Co., c.1850, diam. 30cm/ 12in, **$96–128**

▲ Game tureen by Minton

This large and impressive game tureen was produced by the Minton factory at Stoke-on-Trent. It has the Minton cypher for the year 1860 on the base, plus the mark "B.B.," or "best body," indicating the type of pottery used. This is a very fine example of the "Asiatic Pheasants" pattern; the potting is of high quality, the transfer crisp and clear, and the glaze thick and glossy. Minton began to mark its wares from 1820; year cyphers were introduced in 1842.

Game tureen by Minton, 1860, diam. 35cm/14in, **$320–400**

▼ Small platter

This small platter or game dish is much heavier and of poorer quality than the game tureen shown left. The joins in the transfer are plainly visible, the glaze is thin and the pottery porous, with the result that meat juices have seeped under the glaze. Platters such as this were made in sets of graduated sizes for game, meat and fish. This piece has straight edges, but more interesting wavy-edged examples can be found.

Small platter, 1850, l. 30cm/12in, **$32–48**

Soup plate by Brownhills Pottery Co., c.1880, diam. 28cm/11in, **$24–64**

▲ Soup plate

This soup plate is well potted, with a crisp grey-blue pattern, and a shiny glaze. It was made by the Brownhills Pottery Co., of Staffordshire, between 1872 and 1890. At this period, soup plates were quite large in size, and held up to 300ml/½ pint of liquid. In most kitchens a stock pot for soup could be found simmering on the stove. The soup was high in fat content, and, on poor-quality plates, the fat often leaked under the glaze, staining the pottery. Soup plates tend to be less scratched than dinner plates, as they were used with spoons, rather than knives and forks.

Salt-cellar, c.1880, diam. 7.5cm/3in, **$80–152**

▲ Salt-cellar

Salt-cellars from this period are not very common, as, along with other small items, they were often lost when family homes were divided up. One salt-cellar was shared between four and six people, and there four of them in a service. This example shows part of the main "Asiatic Pheasants" pattern: a pheasant and some of the flowers. There is no border pattern on either the foot or the inner rim.

MARKS

This mark, showing the "Asiatic Pheasants" name in a cartouche, was used by Brownhills Pottery Co., of Tunstall, Staffordshire, between 1872 and 1896.

"Asiatic Pheasants" pattern ~ 17

Animal subjects

Animals are well represented on blue-and-white pottery. One of the earliest examples was produced by Spode, and other potteries, around the beginning of the 19thC, and shows a boy on a buffalo. Designs featuring elephants, camels, and zebras were produced by Rogers c.1815–20. The engravers had never seen these exotic animals, so a certain amount of license was used in their depiction. More accurately observed animals can be found in a series produced in 1836 by Robinson, Wood & Brownfield, showing scenes from the Regent's Park Zoological Gardens, which opened in 1829.

▼ **"Grazing Rabbits" mug**
This charming pattern shows three oversized rabbits eating grass beneath a tree, next to some very large primroses; the thatched cottages and farm building in the background seem small in comparison. A primrose border frames the central design. This mug, possibly an ale mug, holds about 300ml/½ pint. The transfer here is well applied, although, in some examples, the overall effect is spoilt by obtrusive joins. The variable quality of items decorated with this pattern suggests that they were produced by more than one factory. However, the pattern is not common, and examples are collectible.

"Grazing Rabbits" mug, c.1820, ht 10cm/4in, **$1,200–1,360**

"Bewick Stag" platter by Minton, c.1820, w. 53cm/21in, **$1,440–1,920**

◀ **"Bewick Stag" platter by Minton**
This stunning platter was produced by the Minton factory in the 1820s. It shows a large stag in a rural landscape, with three smaller stags in the background. The intricate border is made up of other English animals. The pattern was copied from a woodcut by Thomas Bewick, the famous early 19thC wood-engraver, who worked mainly in the Newcastle area. This pattern is always most impressive when seen on larger items such as this platter, a fact that is reflected in its value. Even a damaged example would fetch a high price, if professionally restored.

"Dogs on the Scent" toilet-box lid, c.1820, l. 17.5cm/7in, **$160–240**

▲ "Dogs on the Scent" toilet-box lid

This lid is from a toilet box, used, as part of a gentleman's wash-stand set, for storing razors. The pattern, produced by an unknown maker, shows a large springer spaniel, hunting for game, with another one behind. To the left of the dogs are two gamekeepers, one holding a rifle. This example shows only part of the overall pattern, which includes a country mansion, a church, and a large lake in the background. This particular lid was made c.1820. It is difficult to place a value on a piece such as this, as it was included in a box of items, sold as a lot by a well-known auction house. Serious collectors will never turn down the chance to buy a lid, as they may one day find the base to match.

"Fallow Deer" plate by Rogers, 1820–25, diam. 25cm/10in, **$160–224**

▲ "Fallow Deer" plate by Rogers

This plate by the Rogers factory, at Longport, in Staffordshire, c.1820–25 shows a snow-covered landscape, with two deer in the foreground and thatched cottages in the background. The border is decorated with flowers, including crocuses. On the reverse, the Rogers name is impressed into the plate body. The pattern was reproduced by Wedgwood in the early 20thC; all Wedgwood examples are clearly marked as such, although pieces are otherwise indistinguishable.

Aesop's fables

Items depicting Aesop's fable "The Lion in Love" were made by Spode in 1830 (continued by Copeland & Garrett 1838–47), and carry a clear backstamp (below). Aesop's fables were the inspiration for many other blue-and-white patterns (*see* below).

"Fox and Lion" plate by Spode, 1831–2, diam. 25cm/10in, **$288–384**

▲ "Fox and Lion" plate by Spode

This pattern, showing a scene from one of Aesop's fables, was part of a series made by Spode, in 1831–2, just before the factory was taken over by Copeland & Garrett, and also produced in green, pink, brown, and black. The same border was used for all the designs. Each size plate has a different subject.

Sporting subjects

Sporting subjects were another popular type of decoration on 19thC blue-and-white pottery. The most famous is the Spode "Indian Sporting" series, introduced c.1820. The Enoch Wood pottery produced its own sporting series, in a dark blue, in 1820, mainly for export to North America, but many examples have found their way back on to the British market. Fox-hunting, gamekeeping, fishing, and other country pursuits are frequently depicted, and the Scottish potter Bell produced a series showing subjects such as badger-baiting. The cruel nature of many of these subjects tends to limit interest to a relatively small number of specialist collectors.

▼ **"Grooms Leading Out" tea plate by Spode**
This plate, from the "Indian Sporting" series, by Spode, shows horses being led out by their grooms. The patterns in the series were taken from the book *Oriental Field Sports* by Captain Thomas Williamson. This is one of the less violent views. Plates of this size were produced in fewer numbers than the larger dinner or soup plates, and, as small items are easily lost, they are relatively uncommon today. The border shows a range of exotic animals. The series was copied in 1842 by the Edward Challinor pottery.

"Grooms Leading Out" tea plate by Spode, c.1820, diam. 15cm/6in, **$320–400**

▲ **"Death of the Bear" dinner plate by Spode**
One of the most common of the Spode "Indian Sporting" series, this pattern shows a huntsman spearing a cornered bear, watched by spectators on an elephant. A dog can be seen in the foreground. This view was used on dinner, soup, and warming plates, and is found on fluted dessert dishes. The border is the same as on the tea plate (left).

"Death of the Bear" dinner plate by Spode, c.1820, diam. 25cm/10in, **$224–320**

"Coursing" dinner plate by Toft & May

This unusual plate comes from a series, showing scenes of hare-coursing, produced by the Toft & May factory, between 1825 and 1829, at Hanley, in Staffordshire. Note that this plate does not have a true border; the pattern extends to the edge. Examples of this series are not common, and not all are marked with the potter's name, although the quality is invariably high.

"Coursing" dinner plate by Toft & May, 1825–9, diam. 25cm/10in, **$240–320**

"Hawking" game dish by Robert Heron

This game dish was produced in Scotland, by Robert Heron's Fife pottery. The main pattern shows two figures on horseback, bending over a third figure with a hawk tethered to his arm. In the background is a castle. The border shows small vignettes of feathers, and a soldier holding a rifle and a dog. This piece was produced in the second half of the 19thC, and, like much work of the period, has far more white surrounding the central pattern than is seen in earlier blue-and-white pottery. Examples of this pattern are most often found in Scotland.

"Hawking" game dish by Robert Heron,1850–1899, diam. 35cm/14in, **$240–288**

"The Chase" breakfast plate by Mills & Fradley, c.1850, diam. 26.5cm/10½in, **$64–96**

▲ "The Chase" breakfast plate by Mills & Fradley

Mills & Fradley, whose name appears, in underglaze blue, on the backstamp of this piece, was a minor Staffordshire pottery. Here the potting is thick and heavy, but the transfer is clear. The pattern shows a hunting scene, with a large, prominent urn behind. The border shows hunting paraphernalia.

Romantic & stylized subjects

This category covers a multitude of designs, from the early "Net" pattern introduced by Spode in 1810, to Minton's popular "Genevese" pattern, which first appeared in 1830, and continued to be produced throughout the 19thC. The most characteristic Romantic patterns were produced after 1842, following the introduction of the Acts of Copyright, which prevented engravers from copying any registered designs, for a period of three years after they first appeared, thus creating a gap in the market for new patterns. During this period, patterns became much more open, showing a larger expanse of white between the central design and the border. The blue also became lighter, owing to advances in the color-mixing process; potteries took further advantage of this to introduce new colors.

▶ **"Net" pattern cusped dish by Spode**
This dessert comport, in the "Net" pattern, was produced by Spode from 1815, and continued in production for many years. The pattern, which looks equally well either way up, was also produced by Minton, Ridgway, and the Liverpool pottery Herculaneum. It may be described as a "chinoiserie" (Chinese-influenced) style. Cusped pieces, such as this dish, are prone to damage at their points, and this piece has a "rivet" repair.

"Net" pattern cusped dish by Spode, 1810, w. 22.5cm/9in, **$192–256**

▼ **"Basket of Flowers" salad bowl by Minton**
The "Basket of Flowers" pattern, seen on this square salad bowl, is identical to a Spode pattern, called "Filigree"; note, however, that Spode baskets are always round. The pattern covers both the inside and the outside of the piece, making it highly decorative even when empty. This example is impressed with the mark "Minton" on the underside. A bowl such as this could also be used for fruit; it should be checked carefully for cracks, especially on the corners, since damage is not always easy to detect on the dense pattern.

"Basket of Flowers" salad bowl by Minton, c.1830, diam. 25cm/10in, **$320–480**

"Devonia" dinner plate by Minton & Boyle, 1836–41, diam. 25cm/10in, **$64–96**

▶ **"Devonia" dinner plate by Minton & Boyle**

This attractive, and well-decorated, plate was produced by the Minton & Boyle partnership, between 1836 and 1841. Its pattern should not be confused with "Devon," another pattern produced at the same time. The central picture shows a woman and children on the steps of a house. The border is very deep, extending well into the body of the plate, and features arrangements of flowers and swags. The quality, and soft, deep color of this piece are superb, and typical of Minton's output. However, these plates are not uncommon so buy only if they are perfect.

▼ **"Genevese" wash-bowl by Minton**

The popular "Genevese" pattern, showing a Swiss mountain scene, was produced by Minton from 1830 to 1900, in addition to a similar pattern known as "Swiss Chalet". Originally part of a toilet set containing a jug, soap dishes, a brush pot, and a chamber pot, this piece could be collected separately to make up a set. The colour of the backstamp is generally a good indicator of the age of the piece.

▼ **"Adelaide's Bower" dinner plate**

Produced by an unknown maker, "Adelaide's Bower" is a very typical Romantic pattern. The main picture shows stylized buildings and ruins. The name of the pattern is printed in underglaze blue, within a floral frame. It may be a tribute to Queen Adelaide, wife of King William IV.

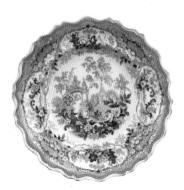

"Adelaide's Bower" dinner plate, c.1837, diam. 20cm/8in, **$64–96**

"Genevese" wash bowl by Minton, c.1830, diam. 60cm/24in, **$160–240**

Sheet patterns

Patterns of this type are so called because they are engraved as one complete, repeating, design, and a single paper transfer is cut from a sheet to fit each object – a very cost-effective way of decorating pottery. The pattern extends to the edge of the object, so a separate border is not necessary. The overall impression is attractive and colorful. Some of the patterns produced using this technique are very intricate; many are found on miniatures, and on items made for children. Other sheet patterns have a definite repeat to the design, creating a balanced decorative style. Many sheet-patterned objects are unmarked, and attribution can be difficult.

Eggcup stand, 1820–25, l. 20cm/8in, **$160–272**

▲ Eggcup stand

Made to hold six matching eggcups, this stand was originally part of a breakfast or supper set. It fitted into an oval-shaped tureen, with a lid, in the bottom of which hot water was placed to keep the eggs warm at the table. The pattern is made up from flowers and petals; a small border has been cut to decorate the foot. This piece is not marked with a maker's name, but dates from between 1820 and 1825. Eggcup stands make attractive ornaments, and are popular with collectors.

▼ Infant's feeding bottle

This is a flat, submarine-type feeding bottle by an unknown maker. It is very well potted, and the joins in the transfer are completely invisible. The pattern is a typical, all-over, sheet design. It is no wonder that the infant mortality rate was so high at this period, as these bottles are impossible to clean. They were produced in two halves, and should be checked for cracks around the edges. The sucking tip, and filling hole, may also be damaged. If the inside is very dirty, it may be cleaned by soaking for a few days in soapy water (use washing-up liquid).

Infant's feeding bottle, c.1820, l. 20cm/8in, **$480–800**

Collecting miniatures

Most miniatures were made as children's toys, and many were lost or damaged, so surviving pieces, in good condition fetch high prices. They should be checked very carefully for signs of restoration. It is also possible to find samples of miniatures, carried by travelling salesmen. These are usually plain white, although single, full-size plates, showing a range of patterns, exist. Some salesmen also carried pattern books.

▼ Miniature platter by Davenport

Made by the Davenport factory at Longport, Staffordshire, this piece is marked on the back in underglaze blue, and also has an impressed anchor, with the date 1840. It was part of a toy dinner service, produced as a faithful replica of a full-size service, even down to the ladles. It is still possible to find complete miniature dinner sets, but at a price. This example is heavily potted, and, like many items made during the 1840s, very white in color.

Miniature platter by Davenport, 1840, l. 7.5cm/3in, **$64–80**

▼ Diamond-shaped dessert comport

Produced c.1820, and originally fitted with a matching set of four inner dishes, this comport was used for sweetmeats or pickles. A complete set is quite rare, and would be worth in the region of $640 to $720. The pattern is a good example of a balanced, repeating design, which has been cut to fit the shape of the dish. In its overall appearance the decoration is white on blue. The ochre rim is hand-painted. This piece is in perfect condition – a rare find, since, on glazed ware such as this, chipping of the enamel can easily occur. The maker is unknown.

Diamond-shaped dessert comport, c.1820, w. 25cm/10in, **$360–480**

▼ "Ferns" tea-cup and saucer by Samuel Alcock

This set, made c.1830, is finely potted, as is most teaware, almost giving the appearance of porcelain. The cup is decorated both inside and out, and the pattern has been expertly cut to fit both items. The backstamp shows a beehive, with the maker's name and the pattern name in underglaze blue. Pieces such as this should be checked for hairline cracks running from the edges, and for damage to the base of the cup and the handle.

"Ferns" teacup and saucer by Samuel Alcock, c.1830, diam. 7.5cm/3in (cup), 12.5cm/5in (saucer) **$128–192**

Geometric patterns

As the name implies, the geometric patterns featured in this section are very angular. Many show a Classical, or (especially on earlier pieces) a Chinese, influence. Patterns of this type were produced throughout the 19thC, into the 20thC, by a wide range of factories. Most were designed as single patterns, that is the same pattern was used for a complete set of items, whatever the size of the individual pieces. Geometric designs blend well with other patterns, but a display comprised entirely of them can be rather monotonous. Geometric patterns are more commonly used only in the borders, especially on Spode's "Willow" pattern, and on early "chinoiserie" designs. The examples shown here are just a selection of a vast range of designs.

▼ **"Grasshopper" soup plate by Spode**
This busy design was first introduced in 1805, and was used for stone china, as the backstamp on this piece indicates. The pattern is very angular, and the grasshopper, and other insects, rather stylized. It was produced with two different borders, the "Trophies" one seen here (composed of Chinese-type symbols) being the more common. The other border is made up of flowers. The rims of stone-china pottery should always be checked for chips.

"Grasshopper" soup plate by Spode, c.1810, diam. 25cm/10in, **$112–144**

▲ **"Gothic Castle" nursery plate by Spode**
Another early Spode pattern, "Gothic Castle" was introduced in 1812. It has an eclectic mix of elements: a castle, a bridge, "chinoiserie"-style trees, a large urn in the foreground, and a border of small vignettes, showing buildings and African animals. This small piece was decorated using a specially engraved copper plate.

"Gothic Castle" nursery plate by Spode, c.1815, diam. 15cm/6in, **$64–96**

"Grape" pattern arcaded plate, c.1820, diam. 20cm/8in, **$240–304**

▲ "Grape" pattern arcaded plate

The dense, geometric pattern on this plate closely resembles a sheet pattern, although closer inspection reveals that the design was not formed from a single transfer. Examples featuring this design are rare, and fetch a high price in good condition. Arcaded plates (see Fact File) are so called because of their delicate, pierced rims, which are prone to damage. This piece has the characteristic basketweave border, and dark-blue rims. It was produced by an unknown maker, and, like all arcaded plates, was part of a dessert service.

▼ "Tendril" pattern game dish by Benjamin Adams

Benjamin Adams worked at the Greengates pottery, in the Tunstall area of Staffordshire. The pattern on this dish is composed of leaves and flowers, around a central geometric design. It is highly stylized, and could even be described as a sheet pattern. Game dishes were produced as part of a graduated set of platters.

"Tendril" pattern game dish by Benjamin Adams, c.1820, diam. 36cm/14in, **$144–640**

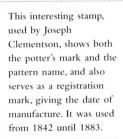

MARKS

This interesting stamp, used by Joseph Clementson, shows both the potter's mark and the pattern name, and also serves as a registration mark, giving the date of manufacture. It was used from 1842 until 1883.

"Classical Antiquities" breakfast plate by Joseph Clementson, 1849, diam. 20cm/8in, **$64–128**

▲ "Classical Antiquities" breakfast plate by Joseph Clementson

The registration mark on the back of this plate tells us that it was produced on 8 March 1849. The plate is part of a series, inspired by classical scenes; each plate shares the same border. This particular design is entitled "Ulysses at the Table of Circe."

Later patterns

Many of the patterns illustrated in this book have stood the test of time. Some, such as the "Willow" and "Italian" patterns (*see* pp.10–14), have remained in production ever since they were first introduced, while others have been reintroduced at a later period. The early 20thC saw a number of 19thC designs brought back into production and printed in a range of colors beside blue. In recent years, Spode has reproduced a series of kitchen sideboard plates, with designs taken from copper plates in the firm's archives; these are clearly marked as reproductions of old patterns.

"Camilla" soup tureen by Copeland, c.1914, ht 30cm/12in, **$560–640**

▶ **"Camilla" soup tureen by Copeland**
This popular design was first produced during the factory's Copeland & Garrett period (see p.12). The soup tureen seen here was made c.1914, and was given to a Sunday School teacher, in 1915, as a wedding present from her pupils. It was used every day, but has survived well, and still retains its original lid and undertray. Matching ladles were also available for these tureens. The area under the lid of a tureen is prone to chipping, and bowls are often found to have star cracks.

▼ **"Camilla" tureen base by Copeland**
This soup-tureen base shows the "Camilla" pattern (left), printed in green. Marked "Copeland Late Spode", in underglaze black, this example can be dated to between 1850 and 1860. Soup-tureen bases, or undertrays, make useful serving dishes, especially for cheese and canapés. As they are heavily potted they are hard-wearing; the most vulnerable areas on these bases are the undersides, which are prone to chipping, and the inner rims, where cracks can occur.

"Camilla" tureen base (in green) by Copeland, c.1855, diam. 38cm/15in, **$144–192**

▼ "Arcadian Chariots" candlesticks by Cauldon

Made as part of a dressing-table set, these candlesticks are attractive ornaments in their own right. The pattern was copied from an earlier pattern of the same name, produced in the last quarter of the 19thC. (Note that earlier examples have a different border, and are a paler blue.) The Cauldon pottery was based at Hanley, in Staffordshire. Matching pairs of candlesticks of any age are quite a rare find, and are highly collectible, even if damaged.

"Arcadian Chariots" candlesticks by Cauldon, c.1920, ht 20cm/8in, **$240–320**

"Abbey" Shredded Wheat dish by George Jones, c.1920, l. 25cm/10in, **$32–48**

▲ "Abbey" Shredded Wheat dish by George Jones

Made in the early 20thC to promote the well-known breakfast cereal, these dishes were available in two sizes to hold one or two Shredded Wheats. They could be obtained by collecting tokens from packets of the cereal. Rather confusingly, the backstamp reads "Abbey 1790;" this does not relate to the age of the dish, but to the original registration date of the "Abbey" pattern.

FACT FILE

▼ "Italian" pattern, Sunlight-soap bowl by Copeland

This bowl, produced by Copeland in 1935, was given away with tokens from Sunlight soap. A matching set of stone-rimmed dishes was also available. Many thousands of these items were made, so they are quite common, and even perfect examples are inexpensive to collect. They were made until 1937, and the month and year are impressed on the bases, which facilitates dating.

"Italian" Sunlight-soap bowl by Copeland, 1935, diam. 12.5cm/5in, **$32–48**

Plates

The most widely collected items of blue-and-white pottery are plates, ranging from miniatures, of 5cm/2in in diameter, to 15cm/6in side plates, and 25cm/10in dinner plates. Collections may be displayed on sideboards, or on shelves, or hung on the wall, although hanging wire should never be used with fine-quality pieces. When planning a display, it is useful to make a diagram showing the arrangement, and including any relevant measurements, for example the space between shelves. Plates make a good background to other pottery, and form the basis of many collections. Follow your own taste when buying, and set a budget limit.

▼ **"Grapevine" dinner plate by Enoch Wood**
Named after its border, which is common to all the items in this series, "Grapevine" is the most extensive of the so-called serial patterns. It was produced by the Staffordshire potter Enoch Wood, between 1820 and 1825. There are different central pictures, showing English country houses or castles. This example shows Fonthill Abbey in Wiltshire. A collection of "Grapevine" plates would make an attractive and interesting display.

"Grapevine" dinner plate by Enoch Wood, 1820–25, diam. 25cm/10in, **$320–400**

▲ **"College Views" soup plate by J. & W. Ridgway**
Pembroke Hall, Cambridge, is depicted on the front of this soup plate, which is one of a series of different-sized plates, showing Oxbridge colleges (see Fact File). The border, featuring a medallion of a goat and cherubs, is common to every item. The backstamp identifies the college. Many colleges are represented in this series, and individual items make good graduation presents.

"College Views" soup plate by J. & W. Ridgway, c.1820, diam 25cm/10in, **$160–240**

▼ "Crown, Acorn and Oak Leaf" soup plate by Meir

Another series named after its border, "Crown, Acorn and Oak Leaf" was produced c.1825 by the Staffordshire potter Meir. There are at least 20 patterns, and although the colors, and quality of the glaze, vary from item to item, the transfers are usually crisp. The central picture on this plate, showing Lampton Hall, Durham, was also used by Enoch Wood for a platter in the "Grapevine" series (see far left).

"Crown, Acorn and Oak Leaf" soup plate by Meir, c.1825, diam. 28cm/11in, **$560–640**

▼ "Beaded Frame" dinner plate by William Mason

This plate, showing Linlithgow Palace, in West Lothian, was produced by William Mason, of Lane Delph, Staffordshire, in 1820. The series name comes from the oblong frame of small beads, on the reverse of the plates, outlining the name of the place shown. The borders, which are the same for all items, show flowers and leaves. Plates are pale to medium blue in color, and some have an enamel overpainting in pink, yellow, and green around the border. This unusual decoration, known as "clobbering," is done by hand after the item is fired. It is prone to chipping and flaking, especially if the plates are stacked.

"Beaded Frame" dinner plate by William Mason, 1820, diam. 25cm/10in, **$160–240**

"College Views" series

- Series produced by John and William Ridgway, of Hanley, Staffordshire, in 1820.
- Over 20 views of Oxbridge colleges, each with the same border.
- Soup tureens, bases, and lids all show different views.
- Backstamp gives name of college, although some were incorrectly marked by illiterate workers.

"Cathedral" dinner plate by Thomas & John Carey, c.1830, diam 25cm/10in, **$208–272**

▲ "Cathedral" series dinner plate by Thomas & John Carey

This rare series appeared between 1823 and 1842, and shows various British cathedrals, in this case Lichfield. Items are light-blue in color, with clear transfers. The borders are decorated with motifs, showing a bishop's miter with a Tudor rose in the centre.

▼ "Antique Scenery" soup plate

A maker has so far not been attributed to this series, which was produced between 1830 and 1835. Examples are fairly common, and show views of the British Isles, this one being Kirkstall Abbey, in Yorkshire. The color on most examples is pale to medium blue, although some are almost gray. "Antique Scenery" uses the same designs on plates and soup plates, unlike some other serial patterns. The backstamp is an underglaze crown, above an oval knot, which outlines the pattern name.

"Antique Scenery" soup plate, c.1830, diam. 25cm/10in, **$128–160**

▼ "Beauties of America" dinner plate by J. & W. Ridgway

This series, which dates from c.1820, was made for the North American market, and is not often found in the UK. The dark-blue pattern was popular with early 19thC, North American buyers. This view shows City Hall, New York; others in the series include Boston State House, versions of which were also produced by Rogers.

"Beauties of America" dinner plate by J. & W. Ridgway, c.1820, diam. 25cm/10in, **$288–384**

▼ "Eastern Street Scene" dinner plate by John & Richard Riley

The central picture on this plate, called "Eastern Street Scene," is a composite pattern. The transfer was originally taken from two prints by Thomas and William Daniel (see p.35), on whose work this series is based. On the left-hand side is the sacred tree of the Hindus, at Gyah Bahar; the buildings on the right are from Chiptore Road, in Calcutta. The same pattern was used for a wide range of items. Perfect examples are quite easy to find; damaged pieces should be avoided.

"Eastern Street Scene" dinner plate by John & Richard Riley, c.1820, diam. 25cm/10in, **$128–192**

"Dr Syntax" dinner plate by Clews

First produced in 1820, mainly for the North American market, this very amusing series features the antics of Dr Syntax. There are 32 views in total, taken from drawings by Thomas Rowlandson, published between 1809 and 1811. This particular design is "Dr Syntax Mistaking a Gentleman's House for an Inn" and is marked "Clews." The "Dr Syntax" series was reproduced in the late 19thC, in a more purplish blue; items are not marked as Clews. All designs in the series are identified on the back, in underglaze blue.

"Dr Syntax" dinner plate by Clews, c.1820, diam. 25cm/10in, **$288–400**

▼ "Union Border" dinner plate by John & Richard Riley

Decorated in a pale blue, this series is identifiable by its border of roses, thistles, and shamrocks, which represent England, Scotland, and Ireland, the three countries joined by the 1800 Act of Union (hence the series name). The central pictures show farmyard scenes. Individual items are not always marked with the maker's name.

"Union Border" dinner plate by John & Richard Riley, c.1830, diam. 20cm/8in, **$128–192**

"Beauties of America"

All items in this series are backstamped, with the series, pattern, and maker's name (City Hall, New York, shown below). There are approximately 23 views, which include the Capitol, Washington (on a platter), and the Almshouse, Boston (on a tureen).

▼ "Byron Gallery Manfred" plate

This rather unusual plate, which was acquired by the author from a dealer in Ireland, has the inscription "Byron Gallery Manfred" on the reverse, but no maker's name. It shows a scene from the narrative poem *Manfred* by Byron. The center is transferred in brown, with a decorative pale-blue border. The style suggests a date of between 1830 and 1840. This piece is almost certainly part of a series based on Byron's poems, but other patterns have so far proved elusive.

"Byron Gallery Manfred" plate, 1830–40, diam. 20cm/8in, **$112–144**

Platters

Platters, or "ashets", as the Scots call them, are the large flat serving dishes that form part of a dinner service. They were available in graduated sizes, from 23cm/9in in width; larger examples (usually 61cm/24in wide) were sometimes available, in sizes up to 71cm/28in, by special order. Platters cover a vast price range, as some patterns are very rare. Each service had only one or, at the most, two sets, so the number of platters made was far smaller than the number of plates produced. A large platter provides a good starting-point to any collection. However, be sure to measure the space between your sideboard shelves before you buy. Alternatively, special, large-size wire hangers, which do not damage the plate, are available, but be very sure that the wall fixing is secure first.

▼ "Monopteros" pattern platter by Rogers
The design on this large platter is repeated on all items in the service. The original pattern was engraved from a Daniel print (see Fact File), called *The Remains of an Ancient Building Near Firoz Shah's Cotilla Delhi*. The pattern was also produced by the Bevington Swansea factory. There are slight variations to the design. In this example there is no border, and the pattern extends to the edge. Prices depend on sizes.

"Monopteros" pattern platter by Rogers, c.1815–20, w. 52.5cm/21in, **$640–880**

"Boston State House" platter, c.1820, w. 52.5cm/21in, **$1,280–1,760**

◄ "Boston State House" platter by Rogers
This impressive platter was produced by the Rogers factory at Longport, Burslem, in Staffordshire. Possibly intended for the overseas market, it is the only North American view made by the company. The design on this platter – repeated on all sizes – is a rural landscape view of Boston State House, with cattle in the foreground, surrounded by a floral, decorative border. This pattern is quite rare in the UK, as most pieces have been exported.

"Gypsy Encampment" platter by Carey, 1820, w. 50cm/20in, **$1,440–1,920**

▲ "Gypsy Encampment" platter by Carey

This delightful platter is from the "Domestic Cattle" series by Carey of Lane End, Staffordshire (1823–42). It is an early piece from the rare series, made up of about eight views featuring domestic animals. Patterns change according to object, although the border remains the same. The backstamp features the title "Domestic Cattle" on the reverse. Prices range from $320 to $400 for a plate and $960 to $1,920 for a platter. Damaged designs are also worth buying.

▼ "Hop Pickers" platter

This platter, and matching drainer, although the wrong size, are very rare, and so far not attributed to any factory. The drainer was used inside the well of the platter, and allowed meat juices and fat to drain through; fish was also served in the well to prevent it from breaking. This pattern (the same throughout) appears on tableware. Depending on size and condition, prices range from $304 to $480 for plates, $640 to $800 for drainers and $960 to $1,920 for single platters.

"Hop Pickers" platter and matching drainer, 1820, w. of platter 52.5cm/21in, **$3,200–4,000** (for the pair)

Daniel prints
• Thomas Daniel, and his nephew William, were responsible for many of the engravings used as source prints on pottery. Both travelled extensively in India and China, sketching scenes.
• The firms of Rogers, Riley, Swansea, and Herculaneum were noted as using Daniel designs.
• Most engravings were published between 1795 and 1835.

FACT FILE

▼ "Masonic Institution for Girls" platter

This rare, and unusual, blue design (maker unknown) shows the Masonic Institution for Orphan Girls in St George's Fields, Southwark, South London. In the centre is the building, built to house 36 girls, with a crocodile of girls to the foreground, within an inner border. The main outer border comprises Masonic symbols. Expect to pay between $320 and $480 for plates and from $1,600 to $4,000 for platters.

"Masonic Institution for Girls" platter, date unknown, w. 52.5cm/21in, **$2,400–4,000**

"Sundial" platter, c.1825–30, w. 40cm/16in, **$480–720**

"Albion" platter, c.1825 w. 52.5cm/21in, **$480–800**

"Combe Bank House/Water Dog" platter by Hicks & Meigh, c.1820, w. 60cm/24in, **$1,600–2,240**

▲ "Combe Bank House/ Water Dog" platter by Hicks & Meigh

Produced by Hicks & Meigh, this large, well-and-tree platter shows a view of Combe Bank House, in Kent, with a water dog, from the "British Views" series. Most of the views in the series are of country mansions, often with a river or lake. The house is taken from a source print, *Seats of Nobility and Gentry in Great Britain*, by Angus, and the dog originates from the source print *Sportsman's Cabinet* by Scott.

▲ "Sundial" platter

This "Sundial" platter was produced, c.1825–30, by an unknown maker, possibly in Staffordshire. Its name comes from the sundial to the left of the picture, which shows two people, and a donkey, within a garden landscape. Overall the color appears to be purple-blue, and, although not particularly common or popular, the pattern has a certain charm. The decorative border is made up of acanthus leaves and pineapples. This pattern is usually only found on tableware. Allow between $96 and $144 for a plate, and $320 to $640 for a platter, depending on the size.

▲ "Albion" platter by J. & W. Ridgway

This platter, which was produced by the John & William Ridgway partnership, and known as "Albion" – a name used by many makers – is another example of a well-and-tree design. A well at one end collects the cooking juices, so that they can be made into gravy. Two or more feet underneath allow the dish to stand level (watch for chips, and even missing feet). The central floral design, an example of the Union spray, is made up of roses, thistles, and shamrocks; the border is a stylized, circle pattern.

"Fonthill Abbey" platter, date unknown, w. 50cm/20in, **$960–1,280**

"North East View of Lancaster" platter, c.1825–30, w. 55cm/22in, **$960–1,200**

▲ **"North East View of Lancaster" platter**

This platter, by an unknown maker, is the largest item in the "Antique Scenery" series. The view shows Lancaster Castle, Saint Mary's Church, and a large, arched bridge crossing the River Lune. The same design, but with different borders, was also used by Elkin & Knight, Herculaneum and Rogers, although this pattern is by no means common. Prices range from $800 to $1,120, depending on the color, and condition, of the piece.

▲ **"Fonthill Abbey" platter by Elkins**

This platter of Fonthill Abbey, in Wiltshire, was produced by the Elkins factory, and is from the "Irish Scenery" series. Ironically, this series contains many views of England, and few of Ireland. The same designs were produced by Carey, as the "Irish Views" series. Any designs showing Fonthill are very sought after by the Beckworth Society, named after the owner of Fonthill. Depending on color and transfer, prices range between $960 and $1,280.

"Antique Scenery" series

• This mark is typical of the series backstamp.
• Although smaller items are not always marked, the name of the view is always shown. Be very careful, as this is sometimes incorrect.

▼ **"Etruscan and Greek vase" platter**

Also by an unknown maker, this platter is printed in an attractive, pale blue, with depth to the color. A large vase, and oversized hollyhocks, dominate the rare design, and the perspective of the mansion buildings in the background is out of proportion. The name of the pattern (probably a serial one) is marked in underglaze blue on the back.

"Etruscan and Greek vase" platter, c.1830, w. 40cm/16in, **$560–720**

Serving dishes

The area of serving dishes covers a wide range of objects. In the early 19thC, food was rarely served in the dishes in which it was prepared. Meat and poultry were usually served on platters, or ashets, and vegetables were typically served in square, or oval, lidded tureens, sometimes with detachable drainers. Sauces and gravy were usually served in sauce tureens, often with matching pottery ladles, and it was *de rigueur* to serve soup in soup tureens – larger versions of sauce tureens. Cheese dishes varied in both size and shape, from the "Stilton" dome, of 1800, to the wedge shape of the late 19thC. More delicate, and decorative, serving dishes from dessert services were designed to complement popular arcaded plates.

"Castle pattern" shell dish, c.1820, w. 25cm/10in, **$240–320**

▲ **"Castle" pattern, shell-shaped dish by Spode**
The "Castle" pattern was originally produced by Spode, and still made during the Copeland & Garrett period. The design was taken from an aquatint by Merigot, *The Gate of Sebastian*. Various dishes, some on pedestals, make up the dessert service. Watch for chips under the handles, and cracks on the rims. The pattern was also made by Clews & Swansea, in the early 19thC.

▼ **"Bridge of Lucano" cheese or cake stand by Spode**
This lidless, low-footed cheese or cake stand was also produced in the 1820s by Spode. The pattern was also produced by the Swansea factory, in 1820, and by an unknown potter, who marked the pattern title in a ribbon on the reverse. Check carefully for signs of damage or repair, especially if you intend to use the dish.

"Bridge of Lucano" cheese or cake stand, 1820, w. 20cm/8in, **$256–400**

"Girl at the Well" soup tureen, 19thC, ht 25cm/10in, **$640–880**

Cheese dishes.
• A cheese "cradle" is intended to hold a whole cheese on its side.
• Stilton "pans" are tall, lidded pans for Stilton cheeses; Stilton (or other whole cheese) "bells" are tall domes, resting on matching bases, often with feet.
• Wedge-shaped dishes were introduced *c.*1840; tall triangular dishes were produced from 1880.

▼ "Girl at the Well" sauce tureen, stand, and ladle, by Spode

The pattern on this matching set, by Spode, was copied by other factories. With a set such as this it is possible to find matching ladles, but be careful to check that the color matches. Look for signs of damage to lids, especially to the ladle apertures. Always view pieces in a good light, and feel for any repairs.

"Girl at the Well" sauce tureen, stand and ladle, c.1825, ht of tureen 15cm/6in, **$640–720**

▲ "Girl at the Well" soup tureen

This soup tureen is the same shape as the sauce tureen, shown left, although larger. On this example, both the ladle and the undertray are missing, which reduces the value. Ladles, with their long handles and heavy usage – soup was served nearly every day – are very vulnerable to damage. Ladles for soup tureens often show signs of wear on one side of the bowl, where they suffered scraping.

"Arcadian Chariots" cheese dish, c.1840–50, ht 12.5cm/5in, **$272–400**

▲ "Arcadian Chariots" cheese dish

Wedge-shaped cheese dishes were not made until c.1840. This small example is printed in the "Arcadian Chariots" pattern (maker unknown). Blue-and-white, wedge-shaped cheese dishes are not common, even though they were produced by Copeland, in the popular "Italian" and "Tower" patterns. Watch for cracks to the lids, especially in corners, and check that the handles are sound.

Kitchenware

The kitchen was at the centre of every large household in the early 19thC, and pottery collections intended for use and display in the kitchen were extensive. Most kitchens had large built-in sideboards designed to display blue transfer-printed ware. Items available range from meat dishes, serving plates, and tureens, to sauce boats and various sizes of storage jar. It is impossible to cover the whole range produced, on just two pages, but the items featured here give an idea of the types of kitchenware available to collectors. Most everyday ware was plain white, especially that used by the servants, but wealthy people used blue and, later, other colors. In those days food was usually stored in cool rooms, or, in larger houses, in ice houses.

▼ "British Flowers" baking dish by J. & W. Ridgway
This open baking dish was made by Ridgway between 1814 and 1830. It is from a series called "British Flowers," and the name is on the reverse, in underglaze blue. As with many patterns, the centers on different items vary. The border shows a Union pattern: a rose, a thistle, and a shamrock. Check for staining, and burnt edges, although both may be removed by a skilled restorer. Never use bleach to remove staining and burns, as it gets under the glaze, and causes permanent discoloration.

"British Flowers" baking dish by J. & W. Ridgway, c.1825, w. 27.5cm/12in, **$288–400**

Wine cooler by Stevenson, c.1825, ht 52.5cm/22in, **$2,880–3,520**

◄ Wine cooler by Ralph Stevenson
In the 19thC, chilled wine was brought to the dining-room, and placed on the sideboard, in wine coolers, ready for use. This very unusual example, which shows Eaton Hall, in Cheshire, the seat of the Grosvenor family, is part of the "Lace Border" series. Although it is sometimes difficult to tell wine coolers from footbaths, in general, wine coolers are more decorative than footbaths, and have pedestal feet, and narrower bases. This example holds eight to ten bottles of wine standing up, or six lying down. Beware of damage to the handles, and marks where coolers may have been used as plant pots. Never pick them up by the handles.

"Filigree" butter-tub by Spode, c.1825–30, ht 10cm/4in, **$256–352**

FACT FILE

Minton partnerships

• Thomas Minton produced pottery from 1793 until 1836, in Stoke-on-Trent.

• From 1817 the company was called Thomas Minton & Son. It was renamed Minton & Boyle (1836–41), changed to Minton & Co. in 1841, and became Mintons in 1870.

• From 1842 each item was also marked with a year cypher – a complete list may be seen in a specialist marks book.

▲ "Filigree" butter-tub by Spode

In the 19thC, butter was made in large, wooden churns, and transferred to tubs, such as this Spode "Filigree" pattern one, for serving. This example is fairly rare, especially as it is still complete with its lid. Four holes are pierced in the top of the lid, to allow air to enter, and the lid is tight fitting. Owing to the high fat content of butter, fat often seeps under the glaze on butter-dishes and causes staining. As advanced dishwashing detergents were not available to dissolve the grease, some butter-tubs have a rancid odor. Make sure that these items are not restored, especially if stained, as cleaning will remove the decoration.

"British Flowers" butter-boat by Spode, c.1825, w. 7.5cm/3in, **$64–144**

▲ "British Flowers" butter-boat by Spode

This small butter-boat, in the "British Flowers" pattern, was produced by the Spode factory. Owing to its small size, only the border pattern is shown. Butter was melted in a saucepan, and transferred to a butter-boat, for serving as a sauce – this was especially popular with asparagus. Butter-boats always have small handles at the back, to stop the user burning his hands. Many are damaged by the heat of the butter, or have chipped handles. Good collections of these items may be formed, as they do not take up much space.

▼ Treacle jar by Read

This unusual, lidded treacle jar, featuring a rural scene, has a tight-fitting pottery screw top to exclude the air. A number is incised on the underside of both the top and the base, to ensure an exact match – otherwise they do not fit. Stains can be removed by soaking the item in hot, soapy water.

Treacle jar by Read, c.1840, ht 15cm/6in, **$320–560**

Conservatory wares

Conservatories were very popular in both the Georgian and the Victorian periods. The size of the conservatory was important, as this was regarded as a measure of one's standing in society. A tanned skin was associated with the working classes, and so ladies, keen to protect themselves from the effects of the sun, used their conservatories as alternative gardens. Special items of pottery were manufactured to furnish conservatories, most of which were copied from traditional Chinese and Japanese shapes. The most popular pieces were garden seats in the shape of barrels. Other items included fish-bowls, lily-pans, plant troughs, and jardinières.

▼ **"Beemaster" garden seat**

Produced in 1820, by an unknown maker, this garden seat, in the "Beemaster" pattern is stunning. The sides are pierced, and the top has a slot cut out so that the seat can be lifted. The "Beemaster" pattern was taken from a watercolor by George Robertson (1742–88), now hanging in a Bedford gallery, called *The Swarm of Bees in Autumn*, and wares featuring the design are rare, and sought after. Value depends greatly on condition, so check carefully for signs of restoration and wear. Any cracks must be stabilized before use.

"Beemaster" pattern garden seat, 1820, ht 37.5cm/15in, **$3,200–4,000**

▼ **"Flown Blue" dog bowl**

As a result of the heavy use they receive, dog bowls are very rare. This example, which is by an unknown maker, is decorated in the "Flown Blue" pattern. Spode manufactured several designs of dog bowl, as did Minton, Brameld, and other potters. Round examples were made, in addition to the shape shown below. Condition is important, so watch out for signs of damage, especially on the feet and corners, and check for cracks on the inside. Many dog bowls have to be restored by collectors.

"Flown Blue" dog bowl, c.1840, ht 10cm/4in, **$640–1,440**

"Flown Blue" jardinière

This fluted, gilt-edged plant pot, in the "Flown Blue" pattern, is highly typical of mass-produced jardinières, made from 1880 to 1890 by one unknown maker. The inside is glazed white, which highlights the top edge. The large, floral decoration, featured here, is characteristic of the late Victorian era. Check the condition carefully: watch for cracks, especially if pots are to be used to hold plants. Line the item with a plastic pot, to prevent staining and seepage from the base.

"Flown Blue" jardinière, c.1880–90, ht 20cm/8in, **$64–96**

"Tower" water-lily pan by Copeland, c.1880–1900, ht 76cm/30in, **$4,800–6,400**

▲ "Tower" water-lily pan by Copeland

Lily-pans were used to house goldfish, and grow water lilies. This two-piece example – the top bowl stands on a square pedestal – was produced by Copeland, from 1880 until 1900, in three sizes, the largest of which is shown. This pan is in Spode's dark-blue, "Tower" pattern, which is darker than the color of the original, early 19thC pattern. These items are rare, so damaged pieces would be acceptable. Check that cracks have stabilized. Bowls and plinths may be found separately.

▼ "Italian" pattern jardinière by Copeland

Another unusual shape in the ever popular "Italian" pattern, this jardinière was available in at least four sizes, of which this is the second largest. The main flower-pot, which has a hole in the bottom to drain water, stands on a matching base. Ensure the base is the correct size, so that the pot sits neatly, with only the border showing. The value will be much lower if the base is not a correct match.

"Italian" pattern jardinière by Copeland, c.1890, ht 12.5cm/5in, **$144–224**

Large jugs

Perennially popular among collectors, large jugs (that is, those measuring between approximately 20cm and 35cm in height (8–14in), and typically made to hold either water – often in basin-and-jug sets – or punch) are both decorative and practical, whether for holding flowers, or simply grouped as a collection on their own. Originally most large jugs were produced to hold punch or water, or as footbath jugs, and very few were made merely for decoration. As the temptation is to use jugs for flowers, it is advisable to buy only examples in perfect condition, as restored jugs cannot be used to hold water. Even so, you may still come across a damaged example that you find irresistible.

"Ponte Molle"
punch jug,
c.1820,
ht 20cm/8in,
$560–800

▶ **"Ponte Molle" punch jug**
This "Dutch" shape jug, in the "Ponte Molle" pattern, produced by an unknown maker, shows the view of a bridge, near Rome, that crosses the river Tiber. It was used to serve punch, and is available in several sizes. Check the tips of spouts for signs of rubbing or chips, as this is the most vulnerable part on a jug of this shape; also check the bases of handles, where there are often firing cracks, which can become bigger over time. Price depends on the size and pattern; some rare patterns can be extremely valuable.

▼ **"Biblical series" footbath jug, attributed to Ridgway**
This Rococo-style jug, which features Jesus with children at His feet, was originally used with a footbath, and intended for use in the bedroom. The footbath featured a depiction of the Last Supper. On this example, which is thought to have been produced by Ridgway, there is an extra handle at the front, which would have helped the user with lifting such a heavy weight. Footbath jugs are vulnerable to damage, and many have suffered cracks and knocks; however, most are worth restoring.

"Biblical series" footbath jug attributed to Ridgway, c.1830, ht 35cm/14in, **$1,440–2,400**

Using water jugs

• Never pour water into a restored jug.

• It is advisable to line jugs, as many are porous and may mark surfaces. Use strong scissors to cut a plastic bottle to fit a jug as a liner. This also prevents staining.

• Never pick up a jug by the handle.

• Use Blu-tack to secure jugs in small spaces, to prevent accidents.

▼ "Lotus" footbath jug by Charles Meigh

This jug in the "Lotus" pattern was produced by Charles Meigh, in Hanley, Staffordshire. The design shows a series of lotus flowers in white on blue, with bands of white between bands of pattern. In this case, the front handle differs from the previous examples, in that it is a projection, and not a loop.

"Lotus" pattern footbath jug by Charles Meigh, c.1840, ht 22.5cm/15in, **$1,360–2,000**

"Blue Rose Border" series footbath jug by Wedgwood, c.1825, ht 35cm/14in, **$1,440–2,400**

▲ "Blue Rose Border" series footbath jug by Wedgwood

This impressive footbath jug was manufactured by the Staffordshire firm of Wedgwood, and is from the "Blue Rose Border" series. The pattern, which shows views of Pembroke Castle, is repeated on both sides. This jug is in near perfect condition, and this is reflected in the value.

"Roselle" water jug by Podmore Walker, c.1855, ht 25cm/10in, **$160–224**

▲ "Roselle" water jug by Podmore Walker

This jug in the "Roselle" pattern, which depicts a stylized view of a river, castles, and figures, is a smaller jug from a jug-and-basin set by Podmore Walker, of Tunstall, Staffordshire. Made of scrolls, the border is typical of a later type of design, having a more open pattern showing more white.

This mark, taken from a "Lotus" pattern footbath jug by Charles Meigh, and showing the initials and pattern name, is a typical Meigh mark.

Small jugs

From miniature cream jugs, up to 600ml (1 pint) milk jugs, small jugs come in a vast range of differing shapes, having been produced by most factories, for both domestic and decorative purposes. Many devotees concentrate solely on building up a very attractive collection of jugs, with prices depending mainly on the condition and rarity of the pattern. On a sideboards or shelves, collections of jugs provide some interesting shapes against a background of plates or platters; however, avoid hanging anything larger than the 300ml (½ pint) size.

▼ Dark-blue jug by Stubbs

This printed jug was made by Joseph Stubbs, who worked in the Longport/Burslem area of Stoke-on-Trent between 1822 and 1836. It was made for the North American export market, where this deep shade of blue was popular in the first half of the 19thC. The pattern shows a boy in period costume, with birds on one side, and fruit and flowers on the other. Peaches and cherries decorate the rest of the jug, and very little white is visible, except on the underside of the handle. Check for damage or restorations, especially around such vulnerable areas as handles and rims.

Dark-blue jug by Stubbs, 1822–36, ht 17.5cm/7in, **$480–800**

▼ "Puzzle" jug

This unusually shaped jug, in the "Two Temples" pattern (possibly of Swansea origin), is known as the "Puzzle" jug, owing to its peculiar pouring method. It has three knobs protruding from a hollow tube encircling the jug's top rim. The hollow tube goes through the hollow handle, to the inside base of the jug. On the underside of the handle is a hole, that must be covered to enable the liquid to pour. Two of the remaining holes must also be covered. Although very restored, this jug is still of some value, as "Puzzle" jugs are fairly rare.

"Puzzle" jug, c.1820, ht 22.5cm/9in, **$640–960** (perfect); **$160–240** (restored)

"Italian" pattern jug
by Copeland, c.1920,
ht 17.5cm/7in,
$96–240

"Crimean War" jug, c.1860,
ht 20cm/8in, **$320–480**

▲ "Crimean War" jug
by Bovey Tracey

This jug commemorates the
Crimean War, featuring the
Siege of Sebastopol on one
side, and the Battle of
Cronstadt on the other. The
names of the battles are
partially printed beneath the
images, but the transfer has
slipped, making them difficult
to read. Cherries, and other
fruit motifs typical of this
Devon pottery, make up the
border. The pottery is thicker,
and not as finely engraved,
as earlier pieces. This example
is more valuable than many
small jugs, owing to the
subject matter depicted.

▲ "Italian" pattern jug
by Copeland

Featuring the popular
"Italian" pattern, this
octagonal jug is in a shape
known as "Hydra," with
its handle in the form of a
serpent, with the head at the
top, and the tail tapering to
a point at the base. This jug
forms part of a set of five or
six graduated sizes, ranging
from a miniature size up to a
jug measuring 1.75 litres (3
pints). Jugs such as this have
broad bases, and are therefore
very stable and practical.
Value is determined largely
by the size and condition.

Marks

The top mark, taken
from the "Fallow
Deer" milk jug below,
is stamped with the
pattern name and
"Wedgwood England."
Underneath is the
earlier, 1820
impressed mark, the
potter's mark, and the
word "Eturia", which
is the name of the
Wedgwood factory.

▼ Milk jug by Wedgwood

This jug features an almost
identical print to the "Fallow
Deer" pattern by Rogers,
although the pottery is whiter
and heavier on this example.
Owing to the small size of jug,
the full border pattern is not
shown. The name of the
pattern and maker are
marked, in underglaze
blue, on the reverse,
with the Wedgwood
cypher. With small items
such as this, only buy
examples in perfect
condition.

Milk jug by Wedgwood,
c.1920, ht 10cm/4in, **$80–96**

Bedroom wares & wash-stands

Before the introduction of bathrooms, in the late 19thC, every bedroom in the home, including those in the servants' quarters, was equipped with its own wash-stand. Some of these bedroom sets were extremely elaborate and finely decorated, while others were made of plain white pottery, or even, in the more basic of cases, of enamel or tin. Most toilet sets comprised a jug and bowl, a soap dish, a sponge bowl, a brush vase, a toilet-box, a chamber pot and a slop-pail for waste. Wash-stands were produced in several different sizes and shapes, and some factories also designed full ranges of pottery to match them. Some of the wealthier homes also had bidets, often fitted with blue-printed liners.

▶ **"Gothic Castle" pattern chamber pot by Spode**
Chamber pots, made for use at night, were usually kept in bedside pot-cupboards. This somewhat unusual early 19thC example was produced by Spode in the "Gothic Castle" pattern – a very stylized pattern, which shows a strong Chinese influence. The shape shown here was made by Spode in many different sizes, including toy and miniature versions. Although not very useful today for their original purpose, chamber pots make very good plant-pots. Early Spode examples may be as much as 30 times more valuable than later ones.

"Gothic Castle" pattern chamber pot by Spode, c.1815–20, ht 20cm/8in, **$320–480**

"Etruscan" toilet-box by Elkin, Knight & Bridgewood, 19thC, w. 15cm/6in, **$192–272**

▼ **Toilet-box by Elkin, Knight & Bridgewood**
In the days when men shaved twice a day, toilet-boxes held dangerously sharp cut-throat razors, on wash-stands or dressing-tables. Two divisions provided space for razors, one for morning, and one for evening, use. The example shown is a white-on-blue style with a matching fitted lid. Some boxes are also decorated on the inside. Watch for damage to the divisions on the inside, for cracks to the base, and chips to the lid.

"Italian Scenery" pattern toilet-box by Meir

The toilet-box shown below is traditionally decorated, in the "Italian Scenery" pattern – a serial pattern that always has the same floral border, but features a different central pattern, according to the shape of the object decorated. Possibly made for export, this example is in a darker shade of blue than usual. These items make good presents, and many people use them as pencil boxes or desk trinkets, or for storing jewellery on top of the dressing-table.

"Italian Scenery" pattern toilet-box by Meir, c.1830, ht 17.5cm/7in, **$160–320**

Round soap-dish

Two-part, round soap-dishes are more unusual than the square, or flatter round, varieties. This example, by an unknown maker, was originally produced without a lid. Most large houses made their own soap, in the form of soft, pliable balls, which fitted especially neatly into dishes of this shape. Shaving soap was also stored in such dishes. The design incorporates large flowers and scrolls, in an all-over pattern. The value given is for a piece in good condition.

Round soap-dish, c.1830, ht 10cm/4in, **$128–192**

The components of a wash-stand set

Wash-stand sets were usually made up of the following:
- A jug with a matching bowl
- A soap-dish and sponge-bowl
- A brush vase for toothbrushes
- A toilet-box for razors
- A chamber pot, a slop-pail, a footbath, and sometimes also a bidet.

FACT FILE

Square, lidded soap-dish by William Smith

This soap-dish, or box, is a more traditional design than the example shown left. The straight-sided base holds a pierced liner, with an inner lip, which in turn holds the decorated lid. It is unusual to find a complete, undamaged soap-dish, although the parts may be found separately. To match a set is rare, but it is a good idea to carry a template of the missing piece with you, just in case. The value range given is for a dish complete with lid. The value is determined, to a degree, by the individual pattern shown.

Soap-dish by William Smith, c.1840, ht 7.5cm/3in, **$280–400**

Blue, marble-effect footbath by Copeland & Garrett, c.1833–47, ht 27.5cm/12in, **$1,280–2,400**

"Zoological" pattern jug and bowl by Robinson, Wood & Brownfield, c.1836–41, ht of bowl 20cm/8in, ht of jug 27.5cm/12in, **$640–880**

▲ Blue marble-effect footbath by Copeland & Garrett

In the 19thC, footbaths were made in large quantities, as mustard baths were considered very beneficial to the health. Made to simulate marble, this footbath was produced by the Copeland & Garrett partnership, between 1833 and 1847. It is fully decorated, both inside and out, and on the underneath, with the blue "marble" pattern. Avoid buying anything damaged in this pattern, as restoration will not be invisible. Today, footbaths are mostly used to hold plants, but the insides should always be lined, to prevent staining. Prices vary, depending on the rarity of the pattern.

"Camilla" pattern hand-basin by Copeland & Garrett, c.1833–47, **$128–280**

▲ "Camilla" pattern hand-basin by Copeland & Garrett

Hand-basin are smaller than the traditional bowls from toilet-sets, and were usually designed to fit into holes in small, corner washstands. Smaller, matching jugs were typically made to accompany them, and these are now often used to hold dried rose petals. The "Camilla" pattern featured here was a popular one, with designs produced in pink and green, in addition to blue.

▲ "Zoological" pattern jug and bowl by Robinson, Wood & Brownfield

This elegant jug and bowl, in the "Zoological" pattern, shows scenes from the Zoological Gardens, in Regent's Park in London. A zebra, and birds in an aviary, are featured on the jug, while the bowl shows a lion in a cage, with plaid-style design around the border. Complete with Rococo handles, the shape of the jug is tall and slender; the bowl, in a softer, pale blue, has a slightly fluted edge, which adds interest and value. The value given is for a piece in perfect condition.

"Morea" pattern wash-bowl by Thomas Dimmock, c.1840, w. 40cm/16in, **$128–192**

▲ "Morea" pattern wash-bowl by Thomas Dimmock

This bowl, made by Thomas Dimmock, a potter from Hanley, in Staffordshire is in the "Morea" pattern (named after a peninsula in Southern Greece), which shows a building, set in a landscape, with a dark-blue, floral border. The shape of the bowl suggests that it was made to sit inside a wash-stand. On the base are the initials "TD," entwined together, with "Morea" printed in blue. Collectors wishing to build up sets should rest assured: it is always possible to find matching jugs.

"Mycene" pattern chamber pot by William Adderley, 1880, ht 20cm/8in, **$112–224**

▲ "Mycene" pattern chamber pot by William Adderley

A later chamber pot than the one shown earlier (see p.48), this piece was made by the William Adderley partnership, in Longton, Staffordshire. At the time Mycene, after which the pattern was named, was the capital of Morea. Many of the later, romantic designs take their names from known places, although they bear no resemblance to them. Heavier, and with larger areas of white than earlier designs, "Mycene" is a typical late 19thC pattern.

Art Nouveau washbowl, c.1900, ht 17.5cm/7in, **$144–240**

▲ Art Nouveau washbowl

Produced at the turn of the century, by an unknown maker, this washbowl is much larger, and more shallow, than the others featured in this section. Its pattern is characteristic of the open, clean style of the post-Victorian era. The matching jug was tall, slender, and elegant. A useful tip: to check that the bowl is the correct match, lay the jug on its side in it. If it is a correct match, the jug will fit neatly into the bowl.

Nursery wares

Even the smaller households had nurseries, nannies, and possibly also governesses, to care for and teach the children of the family. Children were presented to their parents, clean, tidy, and well dressed, only at a certain time of the day, so much of their time was spent in the nursery. Ceramics made specifically for the nursery, and for children, are a vast subject, and a collection may be made from these wares alone. Items available to collectors include special plates, decorated with nursery pictures, mottos, the alphabet, and numerals. The examples illustrated are typical of the more standard, blue-printed nursery wares.

"Dresden Flowers" pattern, toy tea-set by Minton, c.1830, teapot **$80–96**, sucrier **$48–80**, cup and saucer **$56–72**

▲ **"Dresden Flowers" pattern, toy tea-set by Minton**
This part toy tea-set, consisting of a jug, a sucrier (for sugar), and a cup and saucer, would originally have included a teapot, a slop basin and six cups, saucers, and plates. Items such as these may be found individually, so a full set can be built up over time. The price of tea-sets may seem high, but many were broken, as they were made for children to play with.

▼ **Infant's feeding bottle by Ridgway**
Most infants in the early 19thC were breast fed, and they survived in greater numbers than those who were fed from such unhygienic baby feeders as the one shown, which would have been hard to clean. The flat, "submarine" shape has a small hole at one end for the baby to suck and a small hole on top that can be filled with milk. This bottle is from Ridgway's "Humphrey's Clock" series, taken from Charles Dickens' *Tales of the Old Curiosity Shop*, and it shows Little Nell by the riverside. Beware of damage to the centre and tip.

Infant's feeding bottle by Ridgway, c.1830, ht 15cm/6in, **$480–640**

▼ "Verona" pattern pap feeder by Minton

This small, boat-shaped vessel was made to contain pap, a mixture of flour and water, an introduction to feeding on solids. The concoction provided very little nutrition, and was also a ripe medium for germs to multiply in. Pap feeders were used in place of spoons and are available in various shapes; some are flatter and broader than the one shown, others have a half cover at the back. This example features the "Verona" pattern by Minton. Value will depend principally on the desirability of the pattern shown, and the condition of the item.

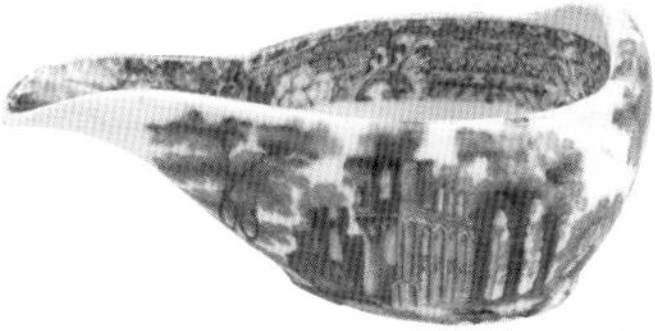

▼ Sunday School plate by Joseph Clementson

Printed in mauve, this small, children's plate is from the Westelyn Methodist Chapel Sunday School. It was made by Joseph Clementson, of the Phoenix works at Hanley, Staffordshire, c.1840. These designs were fairly common, and often bore religious symbols, or the names of the particular institutions for which they were produced. This plate is heavily potted, and has a high, hardwearing glaze, which was intended to make it more durable.

Sunday School plate by Joseph Clementson, c.1840, diam. 12.5cm/5in, **$32–64**

"Humphrey's Clock" patterns

• This was a pale-blue series, introduced by William Ridgway in 1830. It continued to appear, on toy tea-sets and dinnerware, into the early 20thC, in a darker blue, with "England" in the backstamp.

• The series shows scenes from Charles Dickens' *Tales from the Old Curiosity Shop*, and most earlier examples show scenes of the character Little Nell.

• This pattern is often found on medical and toilet wares.

▼ Children's "Boy Musician" pattern chamber pot by Read

This half-size, children's chamber pot was originally designed to slide beneath a cut-out hole in a child's chair: hence the rim. The design shows the "Boy Musician" pattern made by the Read factory in Hanley, Staffordshire. A rare design, seen mostly on toilet items, the picture shows a boy playing a flute, in a rural landscape, with a floral border. Watch for chips under rims and for damage to the bases of handles.

Children's "Boy Musician" chamber pot by Read, c.1840, **$280–400**

"Verona" pattern pap feeder by Minton, c.1830, ht 5cm/2in, **$152–272**

Medical wares

During the 19thC, most invalids were cared for at home, either by their own servants, or by visiting nurses, and consequently the range of medical items produced at the time for home use is quite extensive. It is not possible to include every example here, and wares in addition to those featured include lidded ointment pots, leech jars, medicine spoons, inhalers, and slipper bedpans. With such variety of choice it is possible to form a collection that is based around medical items alone, and many people choose to do just that. Some patterns are found exclusively on medical ware and toilet items. Specialist items often look better grouped together than arranged individually, especially if the progress of both shapes and patterns can be demonstrated by displaying them in this way.

▶ **"Willow" pattern eye-bath by Spode**

Eye-baths are very rare and unusual items, and, although hundreds must have been produced, very few make it to the saleroom. The one shown here, by Spode, is decorated in the "Willow" pattern, although very little of the pattern is actually visible. A feather-edge design decorates the border, and the top part is molded. The stem is also extensively molded, and the border is repeated on the base. Price will depend on the pattern and overall condition. However, as these items are so rare, collectors are advised to buy any examples, even those that are damaged.

"Willow" pattern eye-bath by Spode, c.1815, ht 7.5cm/3in, **$640–1,440**

▼ **"Tower" pattern spittoon by Spode**

Personal spittoons were made in vast numbers and varying shapes and designs, as tuberculosis and other chest conditions were common in the 19thC. This spittoon, by Spode, is in the "Tower" pattern, which was popularly featured on any pottery medical items. The spittoon has a fixed lid, which makes cleaning difficult, and a wide spout for emptying. Some versions have separate, funnel tops. The pattern is on the outside, and on the border inside the funnel, while the spout is decorated with an extra pattern. Watch out for chips to spouts.

"Tower" pattern spittoon by Spode, c.1820, ht 11.5cm/4½in, **$480–800**

"Grazing Rabbits" pattern warming plate, c.1820, ht 5cm/2in, **$560–720**

▲ "Grazing Rabbits" pattern warming plate

Warming plates were used to keep invalids' food warm. Double skinned, they have a space beneath the plate, to hold hot water, poured in through a spout on the side, which often had a cork stopper or ceramic top. Owing to the intended use of these items, cracks often occur on the inner rims of the plates, near the borders, and sometimes also on the handles and spouts. This example (maker unknown) shows the unusual and collectible "Grazing Rabbits" pattern, which greatly increases the price.

▼ "Butterfly and Flowers" pattern invalid feeder

Invalid feeders enabled the sick to drink lying down, while recuperating from illnesses. The pattern on this example, known as "Butterfly and Flowers," seems only to appear on medical or bedroom items. When buying, check for damage to the spouts; the ends should be smooth and glazed, so beware of examples on which the ends have been filed down, to cover chips. The top covers are also vulnerable.

"Butterfly and Flowers" pattern invalid feeder by Minton, c.1830 w. 12.5cm/5in, **$272–400**

▼ "Fairy Queen" pattern bourdaloue by Ridgway

Bourdaloues, coach pots, or slipper pots were placed under ladies' long dresses, and used as toilets. The name is reputed to come from Bourdaloue, a late 17thC Jesuit priest famous for his long sermons. These items were made in a variety of shapes, some resembling sauceboats. This one was produced by William Ridgway, c.1835, and features the "Fairy Queen" pattern. The price varies according to the pattern shown.

"Fairy Queen" pattern bourdaloue by William Ridgway, c.1835, ht 10cm/4in, **$400–720**

Medical wares ~ 55

"Ravenna" pattern urinal
by Clyde Pottery, c.1850,
w. 27.5cm/12in, **$480–800**

"Garden Scenery" pattern,
circular bedpan by Thomas Mayer,
mid-19thC, diam. 20cm/8in,
$480–1,280

▲ "Ravenna" pattern urinal by Clyde Pottery

This rather functional, and somewhat unusual, collector's item was made c.1850 by the Clyde Pottery, in Greenock, Scotland. Although such items as this were mass-produced, only a handful of them appear on sale – perhaps only two or three a year at most. Since these pieces are molded in two halves, check the edges carefully for signs of parting, and look for damage to the rims. Urinals can also be found in other shapes, including some with loop handles. Price will be determined mainly by the overall condition.

▼ "Rhine Views" vomit- or spitting-pot by Davenport

Very similar in shape to children's chamber-pots, these small items are, in fact, pots designed for people to spit or vomit into. Unlike chamber-pots, they have rounded tops, instead of the flatter seat tops. As they do not take up a great deal of room, these pots often make attractive containers to hold plants, although collectors should always take care to line the insides first. The example shown is from the "Rhine Views" series and was made c.1840; the value given is for a piece in perfect condition.

▲ "Garden scenery" pattern, circular bedpan by Thomas Mayer

Also designed for use by bed-ridden invalids were circular bedpans, such as the example above by Thomas Mayer (1843–55), who worked at Hanley, Stoke-on-Trent. This piece is quite rare, as the shape of bedpans (particularly the handles, which assisted in emptying and cleaning, and jut out) meant they were easily damaged. Owing to the rarity of such pieces, it is acceptable to buy damaged ones and have them restored. Value is determined by pattern, age, and condition.

"Rhine Views" series vomit- or spitting-pot by Davenport, c.1840 ht 7.5cm/3in, **$280–360**

"Mycene" pattern vomit- or spitting-pot by William Adderley, 1880, ht 7.5cm/3in, **$160–240**

▲ "Mycene" pattern vomit- or spitting-pot by William Adderley

Another smaller pot, this example is in the same design as the chamber-pot discussed earlier (see p.51). As this pot dates from 1880, it is much heavier, and darker in color than the Davenport example in the "Rhine Views" pattern (see p.56), and is consequently less expensive. These items are more often labelled "porringers," which most collectors find a less off-putting title.

"Northern Scenery" series toastwater jug, c.1830, ht 17.5cm/7in, **$240–400**

▲ "Northern Scenery" series toastwater jug by Meir

Toastwater jugs, which all have built-in strainers, and matching lids, were used in the nursing of invalids. Burnt toast was placed inside them, covered with boiling water, and allowed to stand for some time. The resulting liquid was served to the invalid, as charcoal from burnt toast was reputedly good for the stomach. Any jugs with strainers in the spout should have matching lids. Examples can be found in many designs and sizes; the one above shows Loch Awe.

A quick recap on collecting:

• Always buy what you like, and buy the best you can afford.
• Find a safe place in which to house your collection.
• Buy from a dealer with whom you feel comfortable.
• Catalog the collection, giving the purchase price and date, and note any damage.
• Take photographs of your collection, as an accurate record of what it looks like.
• Add the items in your collection to your house contents insurance policy, and note that the value soon mounts up.
• Read and learn all you can about the subject.

Care & repair

If you are thinking about (or have already begun) forming a collection, you will need to learn how to care for it properly. Items in perfect condition only need to be cleaned in warm, soapy water, but greater care is needed for restored pieces, which should only be quickly dipped into and out of the water, and then gently patted dry with a soft cloth. Be extremely careful when dusting, as handles and knobs are especially vulnerable to damage and can easily be knocked off or chipped.

Repairing cracks

If you decide to buy an item with a crack, and do not want to have it fully restored, place some adhesive tape on the reverse, over the glue, as an extra precaution. Do not use glue on its own, as glued cracks can give way. If the crack is not visible there is really no need for restoration. The plate shown left, which has been repaired with adhesive tape, bears the impressed mark of the Rogers factory.

Staining

The "Willow" pattern patty pan by J. Meir (below left) shows signs of brown staining, from the high fat content of the paté or potted meat that has seeped under the glaze. If an item is not restored, soaking in a hot solution of strong liquid detergent may help to remove such a stain over a period of time. Always rinse the item thoroughly afterward and allow it to dry – this may take some time, as pottery is porous. However, never ever use domestic bleach or chemicals on your collection, and always leave difficult jobs to a professional restorer. If in doubt, seek professional help and advice.

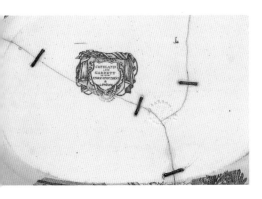

especially large platters stored on damp floors – were often attacked under the glaze by frost, which caused it to flake and lift. Nothing can be done to repair this kind of damage, so collectors should avoid buying such items. The same effect can happen if domestic bleach is used, as it can also cause purple underglaze staining. If in doubt, before treating any of the problems described here, always seek professional advice.

Display

An important part of caring for your collection is knowing how to display it, both to its best advantage and safely. Make sure that items are securely supported, and positioned in places where they are safe from accidental knocks. Old plates are often sold complete with rusty wire hangers, but it is best to remove these – cut carefully through the metal – and replace them with acrylic hangers, which are adjustable and transparent, and do not have sharp points. Acrylic stands are also available and these are practical for supporting items that you wish to display on a flat surface such as a table or a chimneypiece or in a cabinet. Also be sure to keep your fragile blue-and-white items away from vibrations, which might cause them to fall and break.

Stress cracks and storage

The plate shown above left (on page 58) shows the very distinctive backstamp of the "Cathedral series" by Carey. It also has a star crack, caused by stacking too many plates one on top of the other. Plates should be stored on end, preferably with bubble plastic, or other soft material, in between each one. If the plate is restored it is advisable to use an acid-free tissue next to it. Never place a restored item in direct sunlight for long periods of time, as this may cause the color to change.

Rivet repairs

Rivet repairs, which restore damaged items to a usable state, were used extensively before the advent of modern adhesives. China repairers used to call from door to door, and carry out the very skilled process of repairing china on the spot. Items were drilled on either side of the break, then heated, and hot lead rivets were inserted with cement. As the item cooled, the crack closed, and the rivets contracted to form a tight bond. The example above shows a rivet repair to the backstamp of a "Seasons" pattern, open baking-dish by Copeland & Garrett.

Frost damage

The section from a platter, right, is an example of damage caused by frost. Most larders had stone floors, and were unheated. Plates –

Glossary

Acts of Copyright The British Acts of Copyright of 1842 prevented anyone from copying an original design for a period of three year after its registration; this prevented engravers from copying prints, and heralded the onset of the "Romantic" period of new designs

Arcading Looped, pierced, decorative edge found on dessert wares, often decorated in a darker blue; arcaded edges are very vulnerable to damage

Ashet Term used in Scotland to describe platters and serving dishes

Bourdaloue Boat-shaped receptacle, used by ladies under their long skirts for toilet purposes

Cobalt Blue pigment used to color blue printed ware

Chinoiserie Design in the Chinese style, for example the "Willow" pattern

Engraver Skilled craftsman who engraved the original designs on copper

Finial A lid handle, or knob

Flow blue Flowing of the cobalt dye during firing to give the appearance of running; can be introduced artificially by the use of a flown powder

Firing Placing the object in the oven, to set the pattern or glaze

Footrim Raised rim on the underside of an object; does not appear on everything

Gadrooning Raised, decorative edge, often in white, which appears on some designs after 1825

Glaze Strong coating, used to protect the item, which is hardened in the final firing; often has a blue tint

Glost oven High-temperature oven, for hardening the glaze

Kiln Oven used for the setting of the transfer before glazing

Over glaze Decoration applied on top of the glaze after firing; usually hand-painted in enamels

Stilt marks Marks left on pottery by the small pieces of clay used to separate items in the ovens

Transfer-printing Process of decorating transfer ware

Underglaze printing Transfer pattern applied before glazing

Well-and-tree design Serving dish featuring incised channels and a dip at one end, to collect the juices and gravy from meat

What to read

Coysh, A.W. & Henrywood, R.K. *Dictionary of Blue & White Printed Pottery Vols 1 & 2* (Antique Collectors' Club, Woodbridge, 1982 & 1989)

Little, Wilfred Laurence *Staffordshire Blue* (Batsford, London, 1969)

Copeland, Robert *Transfer-printed Pottery* (Shire Books, Princes Risborough, 1999)

Copeland, Robert *Spode's Willow Pattern & Other Designs After the Chinese* (Christie's, London, c.1980)

Gaston, Mary Frank *Blue Willow* (Collectors Books, Paducah, 1989)

Godden, Geoffrey A. *Encyclopaedia of British Pottery & Porcelain Marks* (Barrie & Jenkins, London, 1964)

Savage, George & Newman, Harold *An Illustrated Dictionary of Ceramics* (Thames & Hudson, London, 1976)

Williams, Petra *Flow Blue China* (Fountain House East, Jeffersontown, c.1981)

Williams, Petra *Staffordshire Romantic Transfer Patterns* (Fountain House East, Jeffersontown, 1986)

Where to see & buy

There is a wide range of places where collectors can look at, learn more about, and buy blue-and-white pottery. New collectors are best advised to buy from specialist dealers – members of one of the antiques associations: LAPADA (the Association of Art and Antiques Dealers), and/or BADA (the British Antique Dealers' Association), in the UK, and NAADA (National Art & Antiques Dealers' Association), and AADLA (Art and Antique Dealers' League of America), in the USA – at vetted fairs, such as trade fairs, and events organized by collectors' clubs, and from established auction houses, most of which hold specialist sales. The following list of useful addresses in Great Britain and the USA should start you off.

GREAT BRITAIN

ASSOCIATIONS

Association of Art and Antiques Dealers (LAPADA)
535 King's Road
London SW10 0SZ

British Antique Dealers' Association (BADA)
20 Rutland Gate
London SW7 1BD

MUSEUMS & COLLECTIONS

British Museum
Great Russell Street
London WC1B 3DG

The Potteries Museum & Art Gallery
(formerly City Museum & Art Gallery)
Bethesda Street
Hanley
Stoke-on-Trent ST1 3DW

Spode Museum & Visitors' Centre (The Blue Room)
Church Street
Stoke-on-Trent ST4 1BX

Victoria and Albert Museum
Cromwell Road
South Kensington
London SW7 2RL

Wedgwood Museum & Visitors' Centre
Barlaston
Stoke-on-Trent ST12 9ES

ANTIQUES FAIRS

Antiques For Everyone
National Exhibition Centre
Birmingham B40 1NS
(April, August & December)

British Antique Dealers' Association Fair
Duke of York's Headquarters
London SW1
(held annually, in March)

Buxton Antiques Fair
Buxton
Derbyshire SK17 6XN

Fine Art & Antiques Fair
Olympia
Hammersmith Road
Kensington
London W14 8UX
(February, June & November)

The International Antique & Collectors' Fair
The Newark and
Nottinghamshire Showground
Newark
Nottinghamshire NG24 2NY

LAPADA Annual Fair
National Exhibition Centre
Birmingham B40 1NS
(January)

LAPADA Antiques Fair
Royal College of Art
Kensington Gore
London SW7 (October)

SPECIALIST DEALERS

Antique Shop
136a High Street
Tenterden
Kent TN30 6HT
Tel: 01580 764323

Dockrees
Cheadle Hulme
Business Centre
Clemence House
Mellor Road
Cheadle Hulme
Cheshire SK8 5AT
Tel: 0161 485 1258

Jacobs & Hunt
26 Lavant Street
Petersfield
Hants GU32 3EF

Libra Antiques
Peel Street
London W8
Tel: 020 7727 2990

Gillian Neale
PO Box 247
Aylesbury
Buckinghamshire HP20 1JZ
Tel: 01296 423754

Sue Norman
Antiquarius
135 King's Road
London SW3 4PW
Tel: 020 7352 7217

Paull's of Kenilworth
16b High Street
Old Kenilworth
Warwickshire CV8 1LZ
Tel: 01926 851311

Peter Scott
Bartlet Street Antiques Centre
Bath BA1 2WZ
Tel: 0117 986 8468

MAJOR AUCTION HOUSES

Bonhams Chelsea
65–9 Lots Road
London SW10 0RN

Bonhams Knightsbridge
Montpelier Street
London SW7 1HH

Christie's
8 King Street
London SW1Y 6QT

Christie's South Kensington
85 Old Brompton Road
London SW7 3LD

Dreweatt Neate
Donnington Priory
Donnington
Berkshire RG14 2EJ

Phillips Bayswater
10 Salem Road
London W2 4DI

Phillips
101 New Bond Street
London W1Y 9LG

Sotheby's
34–5 New Bond Street
London W1A 2AA

Sotheby's Sussex
Summers Place
Billingshurst
West Sussex RH14 9AD

NORTH AMERICA

ASSOCIATIONS

**National Art & Antiques
Dealers' Association
(NAADA)**
12 East 56th Street
New York NY 10022

**Art and Antique Dealers'
League of America
(AADLA)**
353 East 78th Street
New York NY 10021

MAJOR AUCTION HOUSES

Butterfield & Butterfield
220 San Bruno Avenue
San Francisco CA 94103

Christie's
502 Park Avenue
New York NY 10021

Christie's East
219 East 67th Street
New York NY 10021

Skinner Inc.
357 Main Street
Bolton MA 01740

Sotheby's
1334 York Avenue
New York NY 10021

ANTIQUES BUYERS' WEBSITE
www.ebay.com
Informs buyers of antiques
received for auction from
many sources, and allows bids
to be made via the internet.

Index

Acknowledgments

Jacket photograph and picture p.2 by Steve Tanner © Octopus Publishing Group Ltd. All other pictures taken by A.J. Photographics © Octopus Publishing Group Ltd, courtesy of Gillian Neale, except: 43 centre and 54 left © Gillian Neale, photograph by Roy Farthing. Thanks to the following for kindly supplying items for photography: Colin and Patricia Parkes 17 bottom right, 42 left; Simon Nicholls 18 right, 34 bottom centre, 47 bottom right, 47 top right, 52 right; Stephen Robinson 20 left, 20 right, 20 centre right, 54 right; Dr T.D. Parsons 28 left; Dr D.S. Parsons 29 top. The publishers would like to thank Laura Hicks for her invaluable contribution to the preparation of this book.